THERE IS NO END

THERE IS NO END

Some Observations On Man's

Struggle Against Oblivion

By

WILLIAM WEST TOMLINSON
Vice President, Temple University

DORRANCE & COMPANY
PHILADELPHIA

To

REBECCA SCOTT TOMLINSON
who has been my constant
companion-observer, this
book is affectionately
dedicated,

By the same author

TIME OUT TO LIVE
THE FLICKERING TORCH

CONTENTS

THERE IS NO END

I. PROSPECT

I

PROSPECT

I HAVE OFTEN wondered by what stroke of circumstance I came to be on earth during the most eventful period of human history. You may argue that other ages were happier, more peaceful or brought more enduring blessings to mankind. That involves an appraisal of values. It is a matter, too, of who is doing the appraising—and when.

Certainly a life which began with the automobile and stood in awe and wonder at radio transmission, the airplane, television and the splitting of the atom—and all the major and minor marvels in between—has been witness to a succession of events which, for sheer excitement, must stand alone in the long continuity of civilization.

On the debit side this segment of eternity includes two disastrous wars and is now clouded by the haunting fear of a third.

Unhappily the increasing destructiveness

of war is the sequel to man's inventive genius. We have now reached the point where an all out world conflict would end in a blackout of civilization. What chance has man to avert such a catastrophe? Is the last great event of this eventful age to be the triumph of man's scientific mind over his body and his soul? Or will man by slow and trying processes—through a fortitude of mind and spirit that marks him as the master of his fate—come at last upon his greatest triumph?

My first postwar visit to Europe was not made in search of answers to these questions. Indeed I had no purpose more profound than that of the conventional traveller in Scandinavia. Among the Scandinavians, however, I found a philosophy and a perspective which was at once provocative and sobering. Not that these North Europeans were solely responsible, for I should probably have made the journeys anyhow, but by the autumn of 1952 I had completed five postwar journeys to Western Europe which carried me into no less than ten countries of that continent.

PROSPECT

By the time I made my third visit my interest was as much philosophical as it was physical. I was concerned with men's hopes and fears, and with those circumstances which are the substance of which both hopes and fears are made. I was concerned with the impact of today's Europe on the destiny of mankind.

There are those who hold that the fate of modern civilization will be decided in Asia or the Middle East and not in Europe. To us of the Western World, however, whose roots go back to European soil and who now, more than ever before, are members of an Atlantic Community, Europe is a decisive area of the earth. What happens there happens in an orbit of existence which geographically, politically and culturally includes the United States.

What is the present economic state and political temper of Europe? Which way is it moving? How do its people feel about war? What changes—encouraging or grave—seem to make themselves evident from one year to the next?

These are the questions I am asked more frequently than any others, and they suggest an increasing awareness that the tides of fortune which beat against European shores are bound to exert a direct influence on the life and lot of America.

I would not know how better to answer the significant queries so often put to me than to submit two thoughtful observations, the first set down following my fourth postwar journey in 1951 and the second written after my return from Europe in the late summer of 1952.

The fact that these two separate observations, recorded a year apart, treat with similar experiences within the boundaries of essentially identical geographic areas, would seem to add to their significance as comparative documents. Within themselves they constitute a report of progress—or retrogression. Perhaps too they may reveal a point of view made more mature by repeated exposure to the thinking of many minds.

In my probings of the inner depths of Europeans I have sought out that researcher's delight, the representative citizen—if such a creature exists. To me he was a combination of the man in the street, around the luncheon table, in the school, the church, the workshop and wherever else human beings were to be found with the capacity to think and the disposition to be articulate.

I neglected, somewhat by design perhaps, the politician and the public official. There was nothing more pointed in this omission than a recognition on my part that such persons are interviewed into insensibility and all too frequently are under compulsion to speak guardedly or for effect. In the final analysis it is the ordinary individual, call him average or representative, who portrays the true mentality of a nation.

From the expressions of such human beings, and from the circumstances which formed their setting I have tried to create a pattern of the future of man's most eventful age. I have tried to envision what may be in prospect for us all.

II. FEAR, CONFUSION
–AND HOPE

II

FEAR, CONFUSION—AND HOPE
1951

We are living in a world of fear, confusion—and hope. It is a world suffering from the physical impact of two disastrous wars within a single generation; it is a world now making physical preparations to defend itself against a new and growing threat to its security and its freedom.

It is imperative that the physical bulwarks of freedom be made impregnable and that no human effort be spared toward such an end. It is vital, too, that this be done before the sands of freedom have run out.

I should like to submit, however, that the security of what we call the democratic world is not a matter of physical forces alone. For physical forces, insofar as they may be made to serve the purposes of human beings, are set in motion by the fears, the hopes and the ambitions of humanity in all its varying segments. The key to the future, then, is in the minds of men.

We in America are deeply concerned— and properly so—over what is in the minds of people everywhere. In my repeated visits to the countries of northern and western Europe I felt a deep interest in viewing something more than enchanting fjords, fertile plains and majestic mountain peaks. Beyond such visual experiences I cherished the hope that I might look into the minds of men. Now, if I may, I should like to try to tell you what I saw. Then I should like to contemplate with you the significance of the fears and hopes and aspirations I discerned.

Germany Revisited

Suppose I begin with the Germans, for here are peoples who have played a decisive part in both the achievements and the tragic failures of Europe and the world. Despite its present prostration I am convinced that Germany will play a major role—in one direction or its opposite—in the destiny of human freedom.

I had visited Germany during the days of Hitler, and I first returned two years ago to witness the desolation and destruction caused by his mad crusade.

I entered Germany in 1950 by way of Hamburg. That city is still the second largest seaport of Europe, ranking next to London in the volume of its tonnage. Something like 50 per cent of Hamburg was destroyed by bombing during the second World War, but today Hamburg boasts of being the most rebuilt city in Germany.

This does not mean that the ugly scars of war are not evident on every hand. My lasting impression of Hamburg will always remain that of a giant pile of stone, rubble and twisted girders filling a whole city block area adjoining the ruins of the central railroad station.

I shall never forget that initial baptism of desolation. I had spent the entire day wandering from one bombed-out section to another, and about six o'clock in the evening I suddenly realized I had completely forgotten to eat lunch. Dragging my weary bones into a cab, I asked the driver to take me to my hotel. As he drove away my troubled mind ventured the remark, "War is a ghastly business, isn't it?"

Turning toward me the driver, obviously a former soldier, replied, "Yes, war is a ghastly business, but it will come again—it must! And when it comes you in America will have too much materiel for Russia, just as you had too much for us. Russia has many men to squander and they are better soldiers than yours, but your intelligence and your equipment will win for you."

It was a bit shocking to hear another war taken so much for granted, and I was inclined to discount the point of view as that of an ex-soldier, still under the hypnotic influence of his Nazi indoctrination.

The next day, however, I found myself

talking with a city official of Hamburg, a sophisticated individual, wise in the ways of both Europe and the world. "America is a great country," he remarked, "and you have produced some very able leaders. Yet, I am convinced that few of those leaders under' stand European politics, much less the Rus' sian mentality." Then his face grew grave as he continued, "You have made some serious blunders in your dealings with Russia, and now I very much fear we shall be called upon to pay in blood for those mistakes."

These conversations came back to me as I sat one day this summer eating lunch with a resident of Hamburg who was the director of a substantial business there. "Germany cannot go on indefinitely as a divided nation," he observed. "Our industrial West needs the food produced by the eastern half of our country. But so long as the Russians occupy the East there can be no real freedom of trade or communication. Russia must be forced to withdraw within her own borders, and if this is not accomplished within the next few years it will be too late. For then Eastern Germany, as well as all the satellite nations will be permanently communized."

The West German attitude toward the turmoil of these times is far from reassuring. Whenever the occasion encouraged me to do so I would ask the question: *Was denkt man von dem Krieg?*—how do people feel about war? The answers came back in a great variety of words, but usually they seemed to mean the same thing—"We hope war may not come, but we fear it will!"

Berlin ist Kaputt

I was not in Berlin in 1951; I was there a year earlier, however, and by recent visitors to that city I am led to feel Berlin has not changed greatly over the past twelve months. But my stay in the former capital of the German Empire during the summer of 1950 will always remain as the most sobering experience of my life.

At the height of its beauty, Berlin was one

of the most stately cities of all the world with its lovely thoroughfares lined with architectural and cultural delights almost beyond number. But today, as those who still exist there put it, *Berlin ist kaputt*—Berlin is destroyed—it is gone—it is dead!

Scenes of destruction are always shocking —at least they are until you have lived with them so long that they become a normal and perhaps even congenial environment. Someone once told of the little Berlin boy who spent a vacation period in Switzerland. Upon his return his young friends eagerly queried him about the joys of his holidays. "Switzerland is all right," he replied, "but I did not have too much fun there. You see, there were no ruins to play in!"

The Berlin which met my eyes was a depressing scene. As the airport bus carried us to the outskirts of the city, bleak, jagged walls, all that remained of the buildings which once stood there, rose before us. Entire streets of such destruction hurled themselves into our faces—brutally, nakedly and with sickening effect.

In Berlin I was quartered in a small frame hotel, formerly a sanitarium, in the Grune- wald section of the city. I arrived just after noon and as soon as I was able to deposit my luggage in my room I went to the terrace for a bite of lunch. The headwaiter, I learned, had worked for twenty years at the old Bristol Hotel in Unter den Linden. He was there when I visited Berlin in 1933. That seemed to establish a nostalgic comradeship.

"The Germans are not bitter over the war," he volunteered. "We do want a chance to work, however. You see we have 300,000 men unemployed in West Berlin and that is not good for a community of two million people.

"Germany must be helped to rebuild," he continued. "Then, too, if Russia is to be dealt with the Western powers must have more men under arms. Call them 'police' or what you wish, the West must be prepared to defend itself."

Here I broke in, "Do you feel Russia will start a big war?" My headwaiter friend thought a long time before answering. Then he spoke, measuring each word carefully as he uttered it, "It is not safe to believe she will not start a big war. If she does I think it will be soon. Within a year or two the West will be stronger. If she wants to start a big war Russia will strike before that. It is not safe to assume war will not come." He had completed the circle of his thinking, and I was scarcely more enlightened than I was before I had submitted my question.

The car I had ordered was now waiting at the door for me, so I folded my napkin, excused myself and joined Otto, my English-speaking driver, for a first trip through the rubble and ruins that were once Berlin.

Otto had been in the German Army for eleven years. He had fought for three years against the Russians, had met the Americans in the Battle of the Bulge and had ended his army career in an American prison camp. "The Russians are brutal, fearless fighters," he told me, "but they are not too intelligent They do not think for themselves. The Americans are not by nature good fighters, but they are intelligent and have the best equipment in the world. That makes them hard to beat."

Over the remains of Berlin horrible memories linger, like the ghosts of a tragic and misspent yesterday.

"When I came back from the war," said Otto, "I found my sister and her two children had been buried under the rubble of the building in which they lived. There are thousands of bodies under all this." He made a sweeping, panoramic gesture with his long arm. "Before the war all Berlin had some four million people. Now it has about three." The others had "gone West"—figuratively and literally.

"The Workers' Paradise"

After I had demonstrated to Otto that I would not prove a difficult charge he volun-

teered, one day, to take me into "the Workers' Paradise."

We entered the Russian sector near the
ruins of the Reichs Chancellory, adjoining
which are the remains of Hitler's death
bunker where he and Eva Braun ended their
lives. Now it is a huge pile of stone and pul-
verized concrete. "Do you suppose anyone
ever found Hitler's body?" I asked. "No,"
replied Otto, "I'm sure he and Eva were
never discovered—they must have been
burned beyond all identification."

On we drove into Unter den Linden, pass-
ing the ruins of the Adlon Hotel and the site
of the old Bristol, now occupied by the beautiful new Russian Embassy building. Across
the street stood the old University of Berlin,
sufficiently restored to permit its operation
under Russian auspices.

As we stood before the University buildings I thought of the old German scholars
who once had studied and taught within

those walls, and these lines of Kipling began
to thunder inside me:

"If you can bear to hear the truth you've
    spoken
 Twisted by knaves to make a trap for
    fools . . ."

How much these words seemed to suit the
circumstance!

Here and there, as we proceeded on our
way, we passed buildings identified by the
letters "H.O." They were the People's Stores,
in which East Berliners bought what was
made available to them. Before one food store
stretched a double line a block long—citizens
of the Workers' Paradise waiting with their
cards to buy rationed food.

"The quality of food is bad," commented
Otto, "and there is a great scarcity of it. The
quality of everything in the Russian sector is
poor, and things are very expensive."

We passed the old Opera House, the
Monument to the Unknown Soldier, the
Palace of Wilhelm II, and the Cathedral, all

of which stood in black gaping ruins. Everywhere there were flags and bunting. Long red
banners with yellow letters screamed the
legend *Freiheit, Einheit and Wohlstand*—
Freedom, Unity and Well-being. These were
the purposes of the Communist efforts—at
least they were the advertised objectives.

Along the streets of East Berlin we saw
boys, singly and in groups, dressed in the blue
shirts of the Russian-sponsored Free German
Youth Organization. "There you are," said
Otto, "the only difference between them and
the Hitler Youth is the color of their shirts.
Get them young, tell them what you want
them to believe and they will know no other
way. It was like that under the Nazis."

Flags, banners, slogans, propaganda, youth
organizations—these are the influences to
which the Germans by nature and by temperament are strangely susceptible. It is all
very well to say they are synthetic substitutes
for the real needs of life—needs which, incidentally, are reasonably well supplied in

West Berlin—but I'm fearful that the Western nations are underestimating the power of such pageantry. This danger is particularly significant as it relates to the young people, the citizens—and the soldiers—of a few years hence. The Russians, I'm disposed to feel, understand the German mind and temperament far better than do the Americans, and perhaps the British.

Otto Unburdens Himself

After our return from the Workers' Paradise I took Otto to lunch. I asked him to select the place, specifying only that it be a restaurant where we could get a good hot meal. He took me to a cafe in Hardenbergstrasse. Otto had told me earlier that he could afford meat only on Sunday. When I ordered soup, steaks, vegetables and ice cream with strawberries Otto sat in silent amazement. But I had resolved that such a lunch should be my good deed for the day.

I wanted to know more about the background of this young fellow who had done so much for me that I could never have done for myself. Under the warming influence of a good meal Otto was disposed to talk and to reminisce. He had graduated from Technical University hoping to enter the automobile business. Then came the war—and the end to all his hopes.

"My father," said Otto, "owned a factory in Eastern Germany which made automobile accessories. But in 1945 the Russians took it.

"Even so," he continued, "when my father was young he had a future. My future is dark, and the future of my little boy . . ." Here Otto shrugged his shoulders in a gesture which signified the despair that was in his mind.

We finished our coffee more in thought than in words, for there was no easy answer to Otto's appraisal of the world in which he found himself.

The day I left Berlin Otto drove me to the airline office where we sat together awaiting the departure of the airport bus. Otto lighted a cigarette and turned as much toward me as the wheel of his car would permit. "I hope you have enjoyed your visit to Berlin," he began. Then with a sudden realization that the word 'enjoyed' was not quite appropriate in describing one's reactions to a scene so wanton as that which lay about us, he continued, "Berlin is . . .," here he searched for a word. "A tragedy," I interposed. "Yes, that is it. Berlin is a tragedy; all Germany is a tragedy to which there is no answer.

"We place great hope in America," he continued, "and we want to know more about your country. We'd like to have more of your good motion-picture films. But please don't send us only your old ones. We don't want gangster pictures either for we've seen too much of gangsterism. Send us pictures that tell us about your culture, your cities, your factories, the way you live and the things you do. We want to see your mountains and your American Indians." When I told Otto that our Indians were a vanishing race his countenance fell. I felt like a man who had just told a child there was no Santa Claus.

I found it hard to realize that this man, with whom I had spent four unforgettable days, was a former German soldier, a man who had fought under the Nazi banner in Russia and on the Western Front against my own country; who had gone through eleven years of military life under Hitler, and who had returned to an all but futureless career in the ruins of Berlin. Somehow it seemed to me he might be speaking more intelligently for his people than all the striped-pants diplomats of the realm.

As Drew Middleton said recently in the *New York Times,* Hans Schmidt in West Germany's Dusseldorf and Hans Schmidt in East German Leipzig both have one crowning desire. It is to see their country reunited. Although they have a haunting fear of this very tragedy, they don't wish their nation to become the battlefield of World War III, nor do they wish to be maneuvered into an East-West Civil conflict. For these reasons they view the hazards of rearmament with no small measure of misgiving. It would be my judgment that this apprehension is decreasing in direct proportion to the growing strength of the West.

Now, despite the fact that I have treated an immense subject in an extremely limited fashion, we must fly along to England, a second vital area on the map of freedom.

Britain—After Two Wars

Two great struggles have left disastrous marks on Britain. London bears her wounds of war—and they are vast and deep—with dignity and pride. But these sterling attributes of British character are inadequate to cope with all the trials that have descended upon the Empire over the past generation.

Once the dominant power of Europe and the world, two wars have sorely bled Great Britain, and have brought her close to the point of exhaustion. She has never been self-sustaining, but has had to buy food and raw materials with the income from her exports and her investments.

The wars which began in 1914 and 1939 have destroyed Britain's reserves, impaired her capacity to export, forced the liquidation of her foreign investments, and in addition have witnessed, in substantial measure, the dissolution of her Empire. Whatever may have been the factors and the forces contributing to the present political and economic estate of Great Britain, it is sufficient to observe that today she finds it difficult to share burdens beyond those which so heavily tax her own resources.

Against such a background, let us look into the minds of the British people. How do they feel about their programs of nationalization? What is their attitude toward rearmament? What of the Welfare State? And what does the future hold? These are the questions to which I sought answers. I sought them everywhere—from Westminster Abbey to the East End of London and from London to Edinburgh and Glasgow. The answers came from bankers and businessmen; educators, doctors and clergymen; clerks, waiters, barbers and taxi drivers—and from scores upon scores of others who represent the great cross section of British life. What was in their minds?

Had I gone to England this summer expecting to hear nationalization widely criticized I should have been in for a major surprise. As a banker friend put it, "Even though the Tories had been in power, they would undoubtedly have been forced to nationalize coal and transportation as both these industries had become so burdened with problems that public operation seemed the only way out. Nationalization of the Bank of England," he continued, "has had little or no effect on the banking processes of Great Britain. They have gone on much as they did before the government took over."

The sentiment regarding public ownership of the steel industry is divided, and there are many who contemplate with genuine alarm the proposed nationalization of Insurance. "Such a development," said a London business leader, "might result disastrously for us. Insurance is one of our major sources of income from abroad, and we could scarcely expect American firms, for example, to place their insurance with our government-owned companies, if by doing so they were put in the position of underwriting our Socialist experiment."

Whatever may be the future trend of Nationalization, on this point all Englishmen are agreed—a sizeable omelet has already been whipped up, and in all Britain there are no political or economic miracle men capable of unscrambling it.

From a Driver's Seat

One day I engaged a cab driver to escort me through the ruined areas that comprise much of the Old Town of London, that mile-square section of which St. Paul's is the center. I had chosen my driver carefully, because my interest included a great deal more than jagged walls and yawning basements. It has been my experience that cab drivers are among the best-informed men a traveller encounters—and frequently the most discerning. My driver, whose name happened to be Ward, had been a member of the Royal Air Force during the recent war, and he bore all the earmarks of that select company.

As I stood with Ward, meditating over the destruction visited upon London by the last war, my mind kept running beyond the scene about us. "How do the English feel about rearmament?" I finally inquired. "There are great numbers of English people," Ward replied, "who view rearmament with serious questioning. As you know, we are now engaged in an extensive program of rearmament, and there are many who feel that the cost of all this is money down the rathole. We are not wholly convinced that another war is inevitable, and all these military preparations serve to depress still more our lowered standard of living."

I am sure my companion had not overlooked the preventive aspect of rearmament, but like many other Englishmen with whom I talked he felt that financial and physical exhaustion were also sources of danger which dare not be disregarded.

"We in England are having a tough struggle," Ward continued. "We seem to have more people than we can support. There are those who say the answer to our problem lies in mass emigration to Canada, Australia and South Africa. So far the English people have not been too receptive to that idea. Maybe it's because they are paying for so many social benefits here in England that they want to stay and collect on them."

I seemed to recall that Benjamin Franklin once had something to say about security versus opportunity, but I kept my thoughts to myself. The problems of Britain are too vast and complex to be disposed of by epigrams.

What of the Future?

There is an immense amount of sober

thinking going on in England today, and
much of it represents a definite break with
tradition. One of my most stimulating discussions took place with a London marketing
expert. Somehow it seemed that he might be
an appropriate person to answer the query,
"What does the future hold for England?"
As I recall, I put my question in just about
those words.

The reply was more comprehensive than
I had anticipated. "By this time," my companion began, "you are familiar with many
of the economic, social and political problems
of Great Britain. I am sure I don't know
the answers to them all, but somehow it seems
to me that the future of England may lie in
a union of nations—the Canadians, the
Americans, the British, the Scandinavians,
the Germans and all the other peoples who
now inhabit Western Europe. This may not
come in my lifetime, but in it I seem to see
the ultimate answer to the problems of our
common civilization.

"We are living in the showdown period

of history," my host continued, "and it is only through the strength that comes from close cooperation that we of the West will be able to meet the challenge of these times. The mantle of leadership has now fallen on you in America, and we in England stand ready to play our full parts in helping you discharge the new responsibilities which are yours."

As I listened to these words I could not feel that the British sun had completely set. Their experience in world affairs, their dogged determination and the philosophy they have bequeathed self-governing peoples were imperishable. The British sense of destiny may have been seriously altered by circumstances, but it is still very much alive, and will remain a force of great influence in the affairs of men.

Danger Makes Philosophers

I cannot leave the European scene without saying just a word about the Scandinavian countries. They are on a flank of the European front, and if war should come these nations would be difficult to defend. No one knows this better than the Scandinavians themselves.

But living in the face of danger seems to make philosophers of men. Nowhere in Europe, for example, have I encountered a greater degree of poise than that exhibited by the Norwegians. Occupied and desecrated by an invading army from 1940 to 1945 they know what war is, yet they refuse to give way to the hysteria of it. They seem to have made their peace with destiny. They will go on living; they will seek to strengthen themselves in every possible way, and if war should come they will face it with all the Viking fortitude at their command.

In many ways the Scandinavians view the problems of mankind with an enviable perspective. The present tumult, as they see it, is but part of a great world readjustment, whose social implications are no less significant than its military aspects.

America's New Responsibility

I have covered a vast amount of ground, both physical and philosophical, within a very short time—too short, in fact, to permit a grasp of the full significance of all the experiences I have tried to bring to you. What do they all mean?

We are, in truth, in the showdown period of history. Our world which once included six or eight large powers, any combination of which might seek to hold others in check, has become an arena of decision in which two super-powers are struggling for world mastery. The first of these is the Soviet Union; the second is the United States of America.

In this crisis of civilization the stricken nations of Western Europe look hopefully to the United States. They recognize our vast physical resources; they pay high tribute to our ingenuity and our industrial might; they are almost bewildered by our undertakings and achievements. But with all their admiration of our strength, and perhaps out of their awareness of their dependence on it, the peoples of Europe are asking some penetrating questions about our weaknesses.

They have not put these questions as I now shall try to do, but in sifting scores upon scores of conversations, with friends and acquaintances on the other side of the Atlantic, I find myself with a residue of three vital queries about this land of ours.

First, how mature are we?

In our lexicon are the words "biggest" and "best" always synonymous? Do we regard life as essentially a mad scramble for things, and is our chief measure of achievement to be found in the volume of physical embellishments with which we are able to surround our lives?

Is what is outside the individual more important to us than that which lies within his mind and heart—and even his soul? How would our philosophy of life affect the world entrusted to our leadership?

Second, have we learned self-discipline?

Are crime, corruption, waste and disregard

for the laws of society as prevalent in America as our press would lead the world to believe? Surely we aren't giving a very happy account of ourselves in this respect. Lack of common honesty, profligate stewardship and indifference to the rights of others are serious indictments against a people to whom the free nations must look for help and guidance.

Third, in what do we place our trust?

There are those in other parts of the world who fear that we place too much reliance on physical power alone. Do we recognize that the intangible attributes of men may be as decisive to the destiny of civilization as are the material forms of existence? Do we realize that through patient and persistent processes of diplomacy, education and understanding we may win the minds of men—and thus perhaps be spared the dreadful alternative of destroying their bodies?

These are not my questions. They are, I am led to feel, the deep-seated concerns many thoughtful Europeans hold regarding America. We may not like them. We may feel they fail to give us credit for our real maturity, intelligence and basic unselfishness. But to fail to heed them would be a disaster for ourselves and for the world.

These questions probe the hidden depths of individual Americans. They are a search —a hopeful search I might add—for those qualities of heart and mind and spirit which make for the true greatness of a people.

The way of the future will not be easy. There is an old Scottish saying that if a thing is hard it is good for you. We don't grow strong through ease and indulgences. With men and with nations, difficulty and even adversity bring out the best within us. I am convinced this will be true of the America which has come upon such unprecedented responsibilities.

We are living in a world of fear and confusion. It is for us to add the qualities of confidence and courage. I know of no other way to accomplish this except through the things we do and the principles for which we stand. Therein lies the hope of free men everywhere.

III. SHADOW OF
ST. SEBALDUS

III

SHADOW OF ST. SEBALDUS
1952

I RETURNED FROM my most recent visit in Europe with a more sobering concern for the future of free civilization than I had felt following any of my four previous postwar journeys to that stricken area of the world.

It was not that the political, economic and military situation in Europe had worsened; over the past five years, in fact, even the most casual observer could not be blind to the Continent's many evidences of recouperation.

The end of fighting in Europe left us with a hope born of the depths. There was only one way to go. Then came the months during which that hope, coupled with pressure from the home folks, led to substantial dismantlement of our military forces and installations all over the world. In the judgment of many who live west of the Iron Curtain, that brought the Free World to its greatest point of vulnerability.

But now we have emerged from those years of misplaced hopes and slowly but methodically are proceeding to fashion the pattern of the future. In the shaping of that pattern the United States of America, as the most powerful nation of the Free World, is bound to exert the dominant influence. To come to the critical issue with rude abruptness, does this mean that the shape of things to come includes a war between Russia and America—which of course would involve their satellites and allies—for the mastery of whatever might be left of our desolated sphere?

From Northern Norway to Southern France the answer one hears to that question is the same—"Who knows?" Nowhere in Europe, however, have I found anyone who looks upon war between East and West with anything but horror and incredulity.

Ghosts of Glory

Germany is the most shockingly persuasive

argument I have yet known against another war. In Berlin, Hamburg, Bremen, Cologne, Frankfurt, Wurzberg, Nuremberg, Munich, Karlsruhe—in all of which cities I have experienced the sickening impact of destruction —and in scores of other places I have not seen, jagged, angry ruins rise up like petrified ghosts of the life and glory which once were there. In some of these cities, notably Hamburg and Frankfurt, a substantial measure of reconstruction has taken place. But all of them stand as mute monuments to the powers of annihilation inventive genius has placed at man's command.

Is it any wonder, then, that the former German soldier who guided me through the rubble that once was Berlin bade me goodbye with the words, "Go back to America and tell your countrymen that war is not good . . . especially if it is war within your own borders!" The Germans have learned that. They know, furthermore, that their country could scarcely escape being one of the first battle-grounds of another general war.

It is the fear that rearmament might lead to a new war that lies back of the German Social Democratic party's opposition to Chancellor Adenauer's agreements looking toward European integration and armed alliance with the West. It was this same fear that inspired "Rudy," a Munich cab driver who had explored with me all the Hitler lore of that old city, to remark, "This idea of a new army for Germany, it is not good. Don't you know we've had enough?" All over Western Germany I've heard comments like that.

With it all, the German people harbor a deep yearning for unity betweeen the East and West divisions of their country. They are not convinced that this can be brought about by peaceful means. Still they are hoping for a miracle. Strangely enough, many of them seem to blame the United States for the fact that Russia is like the man who came to dinner and who shows every disposition to stay on as a permanent although unwelcome guest, eating them out of house and home in the bargain.

I shall never forget the German industrial leader who travelled with me one day along the Rhine, discussing as we went the many sober problems of his country. When we reached the black abutments which once supported the Remagen Bridge it was like opening the floodgates of overwhelming lamentation.

"If, after you had crossed the Remagen Bridge," he began, with a note of sad longing in his voice, "and then followed this success with drives which brought about the downfall of our armies . . . if at that point you had only joined with us to help defeat the enemy of us both . . . then we would not now have this Russian problem to plague us!"

How conveniently we dismiss old transgressions when some new offender rises up to outrage the conscience of mankind! In early 1945 it was still Hitler and his Nazi hordes which threatened to destroy the free world.

Perhaps we were exceedingly naive in the trust we placed in Russia. We still must ask, however, if it is sound long-term strategy to join forces with the minions of a vanquished Satan to outflank the devil. There are many in Germany eager to answer a resounding "yes" to that query, although they would add that with the downfall of Hitler his minions became a disillusioned and repentant throng.

Germany's Neighbors

Returning to France this summer, after a long absence, was an occasion of nostalgic expectancy. The French countryside retained all its pastoral charm and the villages, set in a broad green landscape, were like stepping stones to high adventure.

Outwardly Paris itself was gay. Its side-walk cafes with their bright awnings and jaunty umbrellas remained the splashes of color that set off the whole Parisian ensemble. The wide boulevards and stately circles of the city seemed just as inviting as they were when, as a "refugee" from an American troop and cargo carrier, I was initiated into the allurements of Paris back in the days of World War I.

But something seemed to have happened to France. The more recent past rested heavily on her shoulders and the future held an ominous mien. Perhaps the quick collapse of French resistance in World War II still disturbs her sense of gallantry. She is trying to make up for that today in Indo-China and other parts of the world.

It is no secret that France views the recouperation of Germany with very mixed emotions. The spectre of a militant neighbor, one who so recently has stricken her down, is anything but reassuring. The whole world situation haunts her and she wonders, with a keen sense of logic, if man has lost his mind.

On top of all this France faces serious economic, social and political problems. Inflation has reduced the franc to a small fraction of its former value. Food and other essential commodities, now on a level with American costs, are almost out of reach for a large number of French consumers. Minimum wages in France for a forty-five-hour week are less than fifteen dollars. A skilled mechanic, I am told, will earn just over twenty dollars a week. True these earnings are frequently augmented by government grants based on the number of children and other family situations. Benefits of one sort or another account for substantial state expenditures which must come out of an already overburdened budget.

Lack of vigorous competition, fixed minimum prices, and profits for a long chain of intermediaries between producer and consumer—there is one business enterprise for every fifteen people—help to keep French prices high and living standards low.

Unfortunately the financial assistance the United States has been pouring into France since the close of the war has not aided materially in improving conditions of life for the wage-earning classes. An old American friend of mine who has spent most of the last thirty years in Paris, first in the service of the American government and then as a representative for large American business interests, describes the situation in these words: "Much of the money we have advanced has gone to build up French industries and earnings. No particular thought has been given to the well-being of employees.

"To make matters worse," he continues, "all too many business and professional people — manufacturers, merchants, doctors, lawyers, architects, and even farmers—have managed to escape their share of taxation and have thus shifted the burden to shoulders less able to bear it. Because so many in the higher income brackets avoid direct taxation France lives largely on indirect revenues.

"We have made huge investments in France on the premise that we were helping to build defenses against Communism. Yet today there are 5,000,000 Communist voters in France, two-thirds of whom have turned to the Party largely as a vehicle of protest against the conditions under which they must live."

Is it any wonder that the political situation in France is changeable as a kaleidoscope, and that the design too often shows more red than we like to look upon?

"But don't make the mistake of counting the French out," a prominent European said to me one day as we were discussing the plight of that nation. "France is beginning to emerge from dismal years. She possesses vast resources, by whatever measure you choose to apply. In the ultimate destiny of civilization she will play a part worthy of her heritage. Because of her strategic position in Western Europe she will always remain a key bastion in the defense of freedom."

In the war and postwar years, destruction in Germany received top billing. Sometimes we fail to appreciate, therefore, that other countries have suffered as severely, even though their destruction does not always take the form of jagged walls and gaping ruins.

England is not devoid of terrible physical scars of war. Her losses, however, go so far beyond these material evidences that her position in the world, for all time, has been drastically altered. In two wars she has lost her reserves, her investments abroad and her markets. For better or for worse, she has seen her colonial possessions, one by one, slip from her.

For a nation forced to depend on income earned in the markets of the world these are disastrous losses, for they mean she can no longer support the population of her island. "We need to find new homes for fifteen millions of our people," a British manufacturer commented. "The trouble, however, lies in the fact that our dominions want only our young people—those we can least afford to lose."

It seemed paradoxical to hear another English friend add this sobering reflection. "England's greatest loss," he said, "is one that is now almost forgotten. It is the million men who never returned from World War I. Had the physical and mental vigor of those lives been ours, the fortunes of England over the past quarter century would have been vastly changed. We are a nation whose affairs have been led by old men . . . and that circumstance exacts its inevitable penalty."

What sacrifices Britain has placed on the altar of freedom—this Britain which today looks out across a narrow channel and wonders what new holocaust may be gathering there!

Across that channel lie the Low Countries, and to the north of them the Scandinavian states—"the little people," a famous Norwegian called them. Small perhaps in numbers, but stout of heart and strong in moral fibre and intellectual influence. But they too are unsure!

The Objective View

If I were to have sought an objective point of view on the chaos of the world I should scarcely have known where to look for it.

Certainly not in Germany or France and perhaps not always in England. The Swiss, it
seemed to me, would regard the whole situation in somewhat better perspective than
many of their European neighbors.

A thoughtful discussion, carried on in a
pleasant rural nook not too far from Geneva,
therefore, stands out as one of the particularly rewarding experiences of my last visit in
Europe. Our group, gathered about a festive
board, included the head of a famous scientific
research foundation, an American diplomatic
attaché and the director of one of Switzerland's most important banking institutions.
Pretty good brains, I should say, to apply
themselves to this subject we call World
Politics.

Our conversations, which began at seven,
ended some five hours later when the manager
of the outdoor restaurant hinted, most
graciously, that he'd like to have his table-
cloth in time to put it in the morning wash.

The really serious part of our discussion

followed a story related by the attaché—one, incidentally, which is now going the rounds of Europe.

It seems that the Cabinet of a certain un-named country was meeting to consider ways and means by which it might solve the nation's very distressing economic difficulties. After long discussion the Minister of War came up with a bright idea. "I have it!" he said, "we will declare war on the United States. Of course we shall be defeated and possibly badly demolished, but in the end America will pour a fabulous amount of money into our coun-try, and we shall be better off than ever before."

"Ah, but there is one point you have not considered," interjected the Prime Minister. "We might win! Then think of our disastrous plight!"

"There is more to that story than humor," observed the banker. "Instead of giving the distressed countries of Europe so much money," and here he was directing his remarks to me, "why doesn't your country help them to help themselves? Now you make objects of charity of them, and it's pretty hard for anyone to accept alms without ultimately developing a resentment and even a contempt for the giver."

I was to hear similar comments in other parts of Europe—observations which suggested that America's program for restoring the economy of Free Europe was at serious variance with her commercial policies and practices.

"Do you seriously feel," I put in, "that the devastated countries, particularly those adjoining the Iron Curtain, have much heart for spending their own money in rebuilding? Isn't there too much fear that ultimately Russia will move West and take over the cities they have restored?" My questions were heavily "loaded." No one appreciated this more than I.

"What makes you so certain," responded the financier, "that the Russians plan to overrun the countries west of them? No one—at least no one that I know of—wants to fight, and that includes Russia. The tragic cost of war has at last come home to the peoples who live on this continent."

"Centuries ago the Swiss felt war was a great adventure. They would fight anyone anywhere, and at any time. Then one day they engaged in disastrous conflict far from home, not only suffering defeat, but losing most of their soldiers as well. It wasn't so bad until the bodies of husbands, sons and sweethearts were brought back home. Then the Swiss realized the terrible cost of war in loved ones . . . and they abandoned war as national policy. Europe has seen its dead, numbered in millions. It has looked upon its devastated cities with a horror which few people in American can appreciate.

"You must not overlook the fact that in the final analysis, Russia is being exploited by a small group within the Presidium. Make no mistake about it, they are faced with serious problems both at home and in the countries they dominate. By what rhyme or reason should they be led to start a general war which could only result in tragedy and destruction for themselves, as well as for those countries they seek to exploit?

"Of course they will strive to keep the world off balance, and will play one nation against another so long as that strategy is permitted to work. They will try to bleed you in America white. They will seek to exhaust your material resources in every possible manner. But as for openly fighting you, they are the first to appreciate that would be the open road to disaster."

The more I discussed the question of war in Europe, the more I was brought back to the answer with which we started—"Who knows?" No one in the Western World can look into the minds of those men who sit within the walls of the Kremlin and discern the purposes hidden there. Of this, however, the free peoples seem at last convinced—we must be prepared to meet military aggression should it come. So long as we are faced by both the philosophy and the reality of force and intrigue we dare not put our trust in council chambers alone. We cannot deal with the Russian hazard except from strength; nor can we hope to push back the Iron Curtain with divided forces.

The North Atlantic Treaty Organization is the military implementation of the determination of the Free Western World to remain free. It carries with it the hope of economic and political cooperation which ultimately may transform Europe into a community of peoples with both the strength and spirit to resist any lurking assault upon their freedoms.

Double Trouble

But in many quarters of Europe today one encounters a new apprehension, often inferred, frequently spoken. It is one which suggests that the Western World has more to contemplate than the hulking bear that blows his hot breath across the Great Lowland Plain.

The head of an insurance organization in Amsterdam put it in these words: "Holland, in common with the other small nations of Europe, is beginning to see some goblins peeping in at its windows. This assembly of nations of Western Europe, by whatever name it may be called, inevitably will revolve about Germany as the strongest country among us. France will be a factor, to be sure, and so will Italy—but insofar as purely Continental peoples are concerned, Germany is the nation to reckon with.

"Let me make it clear, I'm all in favor of West European cooperation. That is the only alternative to disaster. Surely you will understand our misgivings, however, in the restoration of German might. In 1945 we were freed from that yoke; now we are about to bend our heads to it again!"

Whether or not this thoughtful Netherlander, with an unpronounceable name, had overestimated the hazard, only the future will reveal. Certainly he had placed the long finger of his mind on the most disturbing aspect of collective security.

What is there about this Germany—twice defeated within one generation—that should so arouse the apprehensions of her neighbors? If the unintended alliteration may be forgiven, I would suggest the following—her past, her position, her potential and her passion for order. To these might also be added her pride.

Any nation which has led the world into disastrous conflict twice within two and a half decades is bound to be suspected in the eyes of those who have been the victims of those aggressions. To place the blame on irresponsible leadership may explain, but it cannot expunge the record.

Wars, we may philosophically observe, do not just happen; they are caused. So it is that the position of Germany has been an influence in her most recent violations of the peace. *Lebensraum,* the Germans call it. From the simple standpoint of people this frantic reaching out for more "room to live" is better understood when we note that today Germany's population density is about 200 per square kilometer as against a similar index of 75 for France, and something less than 30 for the United States.

Even before her division, following World War II, Germany was forced to import a substantial amount of her essential food. Now with the agricultural East cut off from the industrial West the need to exchange manufactured products for food and raw materials has assumed critical proportions. We might carry this *Lebensraum* discussion to much greater lengths and come up with no less disconcerting conclusion than has already been indicated.

For example, we have not touched on unemployment which in West Germany constitutes a major problem; nor have we given thought to the army of refugees from the East streaming into West Germany at the rate of 1,000 per day. Germany's position, we are forced to conclude, is not one to inspire tranquility in the mind of any honest seeker for the cause of war and peace.

It is no disparagement to other peoples of Europe to say that the Germans are unsurpassed in physical stamina, energy, industry and the willingness to make sacrifices for the national good. We must recognize, too, that German contributions to science, invention, literature and art are conspicuous in the whole panorama of modern civilization. These, coupled with a consuming desire to rule, are but indications of the vast potential —for good or evil—that so clearly characterizes this nation that forms the great heart of Europe.

It may seem more than a bit incongruous to cite the German passion for order as a possible threat to the peace of the world. The fact is that historically the Germans have chosen order to freedom. The Weimar Republic failed because the peoples of Germany were too conscious of its laxities and its freedom from controls. Hitler came along promising a regimented order, and that seemed to appeal to the German temperament. It gave them a sense of support and internal security.

It is well for us who have lived for a century and a half under democratic government to remind ourselves that while popular rule, by its very nature, is slow-moving and susceptible to many abuses, it remains our best guarantee against tyranny. In spite of its weaknesses we cling to it because its alternatives are so completely unacceptable.

Free peoples instinctively wonder how any democratic government can survive in an atmosphere of traditional regimentation. The Nazi influence still has live roots in many parts of Germany, and one is led to speculate what might happen if some congenial climate gave encouragement to the growth of this strangulating vine.

The German people—and not without ample reason—feel a great pride in themselves and in their achievements. As one views their ruined cities, punctuated by the remains of great cultural and industrial structures, he detects a deep sense of injured pride that a once glorious nation should have been brought to such a state of ignominy.

There are few spurs to accomplishment so pointed as injured pride. For very practical reasons Germany has neglected the ruins of her homes and cultural shrines to rebuild her factories. Her people live crowded together in the hovels of stricken cities, but the industrial regeneration of Germany is little short of miraculous and is laying the foundations for a broader restoration.

Such is the resurging nation with which the Western World is confronted—a Western World which seems to have recognized that a restored Germany is the inescapable price it must pay for collective security.

Impact of Occupation

If Germany is to make her most auspicious contribution to the security of free peoples she must be more than strong; she must also be sympathetic and worthy of trust. It is appropriate, therefore, to give serious thought to the influence the United States of America is bringing to bear on the last-named attributes. What, for example, has been the impact of the American occupation of Germany since the close of the last war?

As I visited many of the cities in the American Zone of Occupation this summer, I was given the uncomfortable feeling that the Yankees had begun to wear thin their welcome. For the most part our soldiers have conducted themselves well, and as individuals the German people find them cordial, generous and companionable. In the mass, however, they represent a conquering army, and no such force can hope to remain popular in the land of the conquered.

The Germans who think below the surface of their resentments realize that had the Americans and their allies not been in Western Germany over the past seven years, a far less welcome intruder might well have pushed into large areas of their country. From the standpoint of economic recovery American soldiers have brought millions of dollars into Germany, and this added to our formal programs of assistance has resulted in immeasurable benefits. Thoughtful Germans recognize this.

But there are other aspects of the American occupation which are provocative of a bitterness which does not augur well for sympathy and respect for America. The Germans complain that the American Army has taken over too many of their fine hotels, resorts, public buildings and homes. "You have taken the best of everything," is a comment one hears on every hand. When, added to this, one observes a considerable number of Americans driving through the streets of German cities in the finest cars this country produces, he is forced to agree that the Yankees seem to be enjoying life to its fullest on the fat of the German land.

When I suggested to an army officer that, as a matter of inviting good will, our forces in Germany might well conduct themselves

less ostentatiously he replied, "Power and
materialism constitute the only language the
Germans understand, particularly those with
Nazi blood in their veins. When they see us
driving about in big cars and occupying their
best quarters they realize they are a defeated
nation. Only in such a way can that fact be
driven home to them."

Illegitimacy, of course, is as old as war itself; it follows occupying armies like the cleat
tracks of their armored vehicles. But there is
an aspect of this problem which is new to the
Germans of today. A significant number of
the children fathered by American soldiers
are of mixed blood.

The head of the Social Welfare Bureau of
a large German city suggests that Germany's
new democracy, with its freedom from Nazi
racial theories, will face a severe trial as these
children enter school for the first time. "They
are likely to have a rough time of it," she
comments. "It will always be remembered
that they were born out of wedlock, and are
the children of soldiers of a former enemy

nation. The most difficult attitude they will
have to face will be that of grownups who
are still under the influence of Nazi doctrines
of Nordic racial superiority. Those doctrines,
incidentally, are still very, very strong."

Resentments have a way of multiplying
and assuming distorted proportions. Because
Americans in Germany are conspicuous,
there is a disposition to blame them for most
of the woes of that country. More than once,
for example, has a German guide pointed to
one particular area of devastation with the
comment, "The Americans did that just a
few days before the war ended in 1945." The
bombing may have been the work of any one
of the allied air forces, but because of our
prominence and recognized power—and possibly because of some Yankee swashbuckling
—we are crowned "Lord High Executioner."

There is another side to the whole situation
revolving about the occupation of Germany
by American troops. Many rich friendships
have been forged between the peoples of our

two nations, and the enduring value of these is beyond calculation. This is particularly true where the Americans have been privileged to penetrate those barriers which seem to separate former enemies. It is through personal experiences in which the veneer of circumstance is dissolved that men come to view each other as human beings with more to attract than to separate them.

One of the chief reasons for my presence in Germany this past summer was the wedding of my son. He and his American bride were married by a German pastor in a small church not far from Karlsruhe. I was impressed by the warmth of comradeship which permeated the entire group of American soldiers and German civilians who made up the wedding assembly. I was even more impressed by the comments of the German pastor, made as we sat together at dinner the evening before the ceremony.

"It is appropriate," observed the pastor, "that you from the new world should come back to the old to forge a union so meaningful in the lives of men. For it was from this old world that your forbears, many years ago, went to America, and we like to feel that it was the qualities of heart and mind they carried with them that made you strong and great. Today we find ourselves exhausted in body, but we are struggling to nurture that spiritual power which is the one foundation of all human well-being. In it lies the hope of our common future.

"Tomorrow," he continued, "as you enter the church in which the wedding ceremony is to take place, you will walk through the ruins of an old abbey. High above your heads, if you lift your eyes to see it, there stands an old stone archway, on the peak of which grows a rugged fir tree. As long as I can remember that tree has been there, growing in strength and vigor each succeeding year. I would remind you that its roots have grown out of something sacred. They are deeply embedded in the spiritual."

I wonder if this man of God in his simple words did not point out to us the one great source of strength, sympathy and trustworthiness mankind is seeking in Germany—and in all the world.

The True Marks of Maturity

What conclusions may be drawn from this hasty pilgrimage through the desolation and the hopes of Europe? Two, it seems to me, tower above all others. First, there must be a leader among the peoples of the world, a leader to help the weary and the weak and to direct and control the strong and unruly— a champion of human freedom, so sturdy, so wise and so patient as to steer the destiny of men into the paths of security and peace.

America has been chosen by circumstance to be that leader. In the world of our fathers, Britain was the power which undertook to hold the world in balance and at peace. But both Britain and the world have changed since then—"New occasions teach new duties; time makes ancient good uncouth."

New duties came to America unsought— almost without our realization that the burdens of maturity had suddenly been shifted to our youthful shoulders. Throughout our lives we had been growing up, aware of our strengthening sinews and dreaming of our day of greatness. That day came—before we were aware of it—and with demands and obligations some of us would shunt aside or reject completely. But we live in a world of alternatives, one of them too unacceptable to contemplate.

There is no denying the fact that America exaggerates the importance it places on ma-terial strength and substance. We are not a people whose only god is money, and who hold that the answer to every crisis is to be found in machinery and might. The tragic fact is, however, that the world has come to consider these as the things with which we are most richly endowed. We are a nation blessed with physical abundance, but if that is to mark the end of our contribution to the civilization of our time, American leadership will be a brief and futile gesture.

To be sure our generosity has been exploited and abused. It has been my observation, however, that most of the needy nations of Europe accept our help graciously and with deep feelings of appreciation. It would be completely unrealistic to believe that our financial and material aid could be dispensed with at this stage in the recovery of the Free World. None the less our friends abroad accept our assistance with no little humiliation, and with the hope that the day is not too far distant when they may stand firmly on their own economic feet. Our policy toward Europe, it seems to me, should be to speed the coming of that day.

We have not always been wise and far-seeing in our ventures into world affairs. As one Hollander put it, "Too often you have allowed your heart to run away with your head." In the give-and-take of power politics we have on occasion misplaced our trust. If we are to take seriously the criticisms of our friends abroad, at times we have placed on the altar of expediency that which was really not ours to give. Such are the errors of idealism!

But we will rise to meet the challenge which confronts us. Free peoples everywhere believe this with deep conviction. To our physical power we will add the strength of wisdom. Then we will come to realize that even these are not enough. There is a force we call the spirit of man—that power emphasized by the German pastor—in which the eternal stamina of mankind is lodged. Only when that dominates the world will human freedom be secure.

I have one great fear about America. It is the sobering concern I expressed at the outset of this discussion. It is that we shall not have the patience to carry through the task destiny has placed before us. We are a people so accustomed to tackling big jobs, seeing them through speedily and then rushing on to the next, that we shall find it difficult to live year in year out with a responsibility which has no end. Yet that is the test which lies before America.

In the devastation of Nuremberg I stood not long ago before the ruins of St. Sebaldus.

Its walls were little more than the hollow shell of a once beautiful religious shrine. Through gaping holes the afternoon sun streamed down on the stony figures of saints, awaiting the day when they might be restored to their niches of former glory.

Before the church a stonecutter stood chipping away at a block of granite, reshaping it to fit one small hole in the walls desecrated by man's most recent barbarism. His face was calm and intent. He was unhurried as he raised and lowered the wooden mallet which gave force and direction to his chisel.

Time to that stonecutter was not important. Only the ultimate goal—the master plan —was of commanding significance. Neither he nor any of the other artisans working on the restoration of that church would live to see their task completed. That did not seem to matter. The important realization was that they were part of a master plan.

Through my mind there passed a kindred realization. We in America have been called upon by destiny to help rebuild a shattered world into a place of beauty and of hope. It is a task not for a year, not for a decade, per-haps not for a century. None of us now living will see our work completed. We are, how-ever, parts of a master plan.

But is the United States to stand alone as the builder of freedom and of peace? This brings us to the second conclusion of these considerations. If we are to be but one stone-cutter faced with the task of massive recon-struction, we shall ultimately abandon the project in discouragement. We must utilize to the fullest degree other craftsmen in the art of building a finer and more secure civilization.

The United Nations was established with such purposes in mind. True, at times, it has done its work imperfectly; it has met frustra-tions which have caused us disappointment and despair. As time goes on we may seek ways of making it a more perfect instrument, but the idea which gave it birth remains the mark of wisdom and maturity. The United

States, it seems to me, should be the first to recognize this fact.

We who are the builders live in the long shadow of St. Sebaldus. Often, we shall need to partake of the inspiration and example of that scene.

Now that I've set these thoughts and observations down on paper and reread them, not once but many times, I am led to ask— do they read like the prescription an international "do-gooder" would foist upon an ailing world?

In rash and unbridled generosity, the realists point out, the United States can so exhaust its strength as to become impotent both at home and abroad. Then the giant of the West would stand weak and helpless before a big red bear—just as the proponents of World Communism have long planned that it might stand.

But the big red bear feeds on want and poverty; he lives on fear, hopelessness and desperation. We shall fend him off and drive him back only as we help to create the kind of environment which he finds hostile to his survival. This is a task for people everywhere who cherish dignity above degradation.

My old American friend in Paris puts all this in five-and-ten-cent words that no one can misunderstand. "The United States of America," he declares, "must support the Free World purely as a matter of self-preservation. It is as simple as that!"

IV. PERSPECTIVE

IV

PERSPECTIVE

IT IS NOT easy for men to view the events of their own lives in the long perspective of history. In fact, one of the most characteristic traits of the human being is his disposition to yawn in the face of those miracles to which he has been witness. They seem to have earned the contempt which is born of intimate familiarity.

These observations were introduced by an abbreviated reference to the inventive genius that has marked this segment of eternity. That, too, we tend to look down our noses upon.

I was a stripling, with a nose too small to look down, when my father, one day, sent out word from town that Tom L. Johnson was about to pass our home in his automobile. Johnson was mayor of Cleveland and he owned one of the first "horse frighteners" in the state of Ohio. In it he was undertaking a

[93]

daring journey of almost 150 miles over the narrow, winding, dirt roads that connected Cleveland with Pittsburgh.

I shall never forget how we kids, and grownups too, craned our necks to catch the first glimpse of that new marvel. Suddenly, way up the road, at the top of the Damascus Hill, a cloud of dust appeared. Then rumbling out of it, at the fabulous speed of fifteen miles an hour, came Tom L. Johnson in a flashing red vehicle no larger than a modern jeep. We watched it pass, then saw it slowly disappear beyond Emmor Walker's grocery store almost a mile away. We had been witnesses to the substance of man's dreams—to the fruits of his daring imagination.

Today in America we have over forty million motor cars—more than the rest of the world combined. They are as commonplace as church spires and frequently far more popular.

As man followed the graceful soaring of the creatures of the air another ambition fired his restless mind. It was that he too might fly.

PERSPECTIVE

Each Fourth of July at my boyhood home we used to view a prelude to man's conquest of the air. In the center of the old race track a bizarre figure, clad in green tights and a flowing red blouse, would push his way through the crowd to a large gas-filled bag. There were moments of careful preparation and inspection; then as men stood tense the great bag was cut loose from its moorings and balloon and balloonist would rise high into the atmosphere to ride the fickle winds to glory. Ultimate glory proved to be the corn field of John Rogers or some other farmer. That did not matter. Momentarily, at least, the air had been conquered and man had felt a great lift to his ambitions.

What a span it takes to bridge the gap between that stunt balloonist and today's keen-eyed pilot whose plane reduces time and space to capsule dimensions. Man has now out-stripped the speed of sound; the skyways of the air have become the pathways of the world and man accepts it all with little more than a mild jolt to his sensibilities. Yet it all falls within the orbit of the miraculous.

One more reflection. Every community, I suppose, has had its Tom-the-Tinkerers. He is the pseudo-genius who never quite crashes the doors of the Patent Office. I have vivid memories of just such a mechanical doodler who was always on the verge of perfecting a perpetual motion machine. And when he succeeded the whole world would have more energy and power than it knew what to do with! Long ago I lost track of this particular human benefactor. This much, however, I know—the world is still awaiting the limitless energy he dreamed and talked about.

Or is it? Only yesterday a group of scientists came upon a source of energy so vast and limitless as to defy human comprehension. They split the atom and unlocked a universe of power. That became the miracle of miracles and one sometimes wonders if the world is not still too dazed to be impressed by the momentous import of it all.

Forces of Destiny

At this point it must be clearly evident that we have been dealing, not with the pigmy playthings of mankind, but rather with powerful forces about which the very destiny of civilization revolves.

Tom L. Johnson's little red automobile has now become an armored tank spewing death from every turret; the balloon that came down so ingloriously in John Rogers' corn field is now a fighter plane that prowls the skies of seven continents. And the perpetual motion machine has its counterpart in the atomic bomb which, in a flash, can visit obliteration on a thousand Hiroshimas of the world. Only an imbecile can yawn in the face of these realities.

On such forces of destruction we are compelled to rely for the protection of our freedom and our security. But these agents of annihilation, we must recognize, have no high and idealistic loyalties. They are the willing servants of him who possesses and controls them. They would be as quick to release their devastation on the free as upon the enemies of freedom.

As we stand guard, therefore, we find ourselves faced with a search for a kind of mutual security which, in the end, will not rely solely on weapons of destruction. The obstacles in that search are fear, ignorance, want, hatred and ambition. For a time force may be our only bulwark, but surely it is not a bastion worthy of the estate we like to refer to as civilization.

On a journey from Amsterdam to Brussels this summer my compartment companion happened to be a very keen Belgian whose business carried him into many parts of Western Europe. We had been discussing man's precarious position at this mid-point of the Twentieth Century.

"It is unfortunate," I remarked, "that the world has been reduced to two great powers and that between these two the fate of mankind is suspended."

"If I may correct you," my companion

interjected, "there are not two great powers, but three, and the third is the truly decisive factor in the rescue of mankind. There is Russia, of course . . . and America. And there is also the Church!"

I had become so accustomed to discussions of power politics that I was not quite prepared for the turn our conversation had taken. I suppose my friend was a Roman Catholic. I did not ask. His subsequent comments, however, indicated that he was thinking of the Church, not as a denominational body, but rather as a religious and spiritual force.

"True religion," he continued, "is a universal power. Neither tanks nor bombs nor iron curtains can silence it. It is the enduring hope of men—whether they dwell in the Soviet Union, in the vastness of the Orient, or in Europe or America.

"The only trouble with the Church is that there are not enough good churchmen to strengthen and uphold it. Man has turned from God to guns and therein lies his peril."

From God to guns! From moral force to material power! How vulnerable, I asked myself, was America to this colossal indictment?

The great longing of the world is not for that which repels and divides, but rather for that which draws men together in understanding and in trust.

We are engaged in a desperate search for an elusive goal—that human plan or situation which will give to men the means and the capacity for living together in harmony, security and peace. Therein lies the undiscovered secret of this age. Only as we come at last upon that secret will man have achieved his greatest triumph.

Such is the pilgrimage upon which America has been called to lead the world. The journey will be difficult and long. It will lead through arduous paths which will put to rigorous test our moral integrity and our spiritual strength. In the great challenge destiny has placed before us there is no end. It will continue so long as those of us now living may endure. It will be our burden . . . and our glory.